SWEET
CHILLI
FRIDAY

WHAT'S COOKING?

What's better than meeting with friends, sharing stories and enjoying good food? Well if you're as passionate about cooking as we are, being able to share your favourite recipes and show your nearest and dearest how easy they are to make all adds to the fun.

We started our cooking group, Peppercorn Passion, when two of us – old school friends Sangita and Sheetal – moaned to each other about how we both always made the same five dishes over and over again. But what if we swapped recipes? We would have ten great dishes between us instead of five. It didn't take long to work out that adding a couple more friends in to the mix would double that figure and substantially expand our cooking repertoire! That thought process gave birth to our "Friday night cook club" so we joined up with Sonia and Alpa, followed by Deepa and Anjana, before we knew it Peppercorn Passion was born.

The idea is simple. We rotate the cooking club around all of our houses, usually on a Friday night, and whoever is hosting the evening will prepare a recipe card and demonstrate three or four dishes, while everyone watches them cook. We make notes with ideas about how we would like to adjust each recipe to fit our own tastes and then we sit and have dinner together, catch up on life, and enjoy the food. We also tend to put the world to rights! This has been going on for a few years now.

We're always discussing the recipes and how we'll tweak them for each of our own families. After a cooking club we usually get home about midnight and by 7am the next morning, we'll be having a group chat about the dishes and someone will have already sent a new version with different ingredients! So it's not unusual to have six different versions of any particular recipe.

Everything we cook is vegetarian (although we are not strict like some people, so where we use lots of cheese, strict veggies need to make sure they use vegetarian cheese) and the headline rule is to keep it simple. We're all busy working mothers so we want our dishes to be easy enough for everyone to make at home on a midweek night for the whole family. We only use ingredients you can source easily or will already have in your store cupboards. No-one wants to be eating at 11 o'clock at night, do they?

The truth is, we're not chefs... we're busy people with hectic lives who don't want to spend hours and hours in the kitchen. However, we love great tasting food that looks amazing too.

WHO'S WHO?

We all have our own style; that's what keeps the group interesting and hopefully, in this book, you'll enjoy the variety.

Alpa's cooking is always healthy so her recipes are full of vegetables and very light. Her desserts are really easy to make but also incredibly tasty. She's probably the most adventurous and is always trying new recipes; she's also the first one to go back and try out everyone else's recipe, so if she hasn't replicated a dish by 7am on the Saturday morning following a cook club meeting, we're all very disappointed! Alpa works as a diabetes specialist podiatrist. She is married with twins.

Anjana (or 'Anj' as we call her) is our 'surprise ingredient' cook. She's a management accountant who has a creative approach to cooking and likes to combine different tastes and influences to come up with something unique. She is passionate about quality and makes a point about focusing on developing the flavours in dishes without always resorting to that old favourite ingredient, chilli, yet still manages to make it taste amazing. The rest of us tend to rely on that spice 'hit' to ensure the food tastes good. Her broccoli and halloumi curry surprised us all – as well as being truly original it's full of depth and flavour, a real crowd pleaser! Anj is married with two kids.

You'd call Deepa's style 'Bombay street food with a modern twist'. The samosa recipe on page 47 is a perfect example of that. We think of her as the Indian Queen; she does everything with finesse, even the way she rolls the paneer wraps. She's also the mum of the group; always fussing, checking on our kids and making sure we all get home safely. Deepa says that the group has given her the confidence to develop her cooking skills to the next level. We all disagree - she inspires us! Deepa is married and has one daughter and two households to run (don't ask!).

Sangita is a bit of a hidden talent. By day, she's a litigation lawyer who doesn't really think she can cook but she's actually got a natural flair for it. She goes straight to the source; so rather than buying a Thai curry paste, she'll start from scratch and make her own. She also likes her rich, indulgent foods and flavours of chilli, garlic and onion. She is very put off by long and tedious recipes with unrecognisable ingredients. It has to be quick and easy but delicious. Imagine Jamie Oliver mixed with a bit of Nigella. Sangita is married and has two very opinionated teenage daughters.

Sheetal is fabulous at making desserts and is a naturally talented chef. She's a mother of three and is an exams manager by day. Her passion for cooking started when she first got married and her husband thought all vegetarian food was boring. It has been her mission since then to prove that it's anything but that. She loves to create dishes by combining ingredients from a number of different recipes and then adding her own twist, therefore creating something new and different. She can make really simple dishes taste amazing; our kids all ask for her cookies and cream cheesecake whenever she comes round.

Sonia is the health conscious one. Her recipes often use lower fat versions of foods like cheese and pastry yet still taste great. Sonia isn't too keen on onions and garlic, however she enjoys using a wide variety of herbs and spices to add great flavour to dishes. She loves quick recipes that taste good and look fantastic. Her smoked aubergine crostini is a great example of this. As the only non-vegetarian in the group, she loves the versatility of some of these recipes, in that they can be used equally with meat, fish or vegetables. Sonia is a chartered accountant and is married with two daughters.

...AND IT'S NOT JUST ABOUT THE FOOD

The fact is, we're all really different people and have diverse cooking styles and that's probably why the group works. It's not all about the food though. If someone misses a session, that person is really missed; we've got this great bond between us. We sit, eat, chat and we gossip, we do the whole lot. What's said around the table stays around the table.

Our recipes are there to be adapted, played and tinkered with. Cooking should be communal... and most importantly, it should be fun.

Nourish

healthy dishes to feed the soul

Griddled Aubergine with Feta Salsa

A low carb alternative to a classic bruschetta.

INGREDIENTS

1-2 medium aubergines

Salt, to taste

Olive oil, to brush

Pepper, to taste

100g feta cheese, chopped

2 tomatoes, chopped and deseeded

¼ cucumber, chopped

Small bunch of parsley, chopped

Lemon juice, to taste

METHOD

1. Begin by slicing off the top part of the aubergines and cut them into 1cm thick slices lengthways. Place in a colander, sprinkle each slice with salt and set them aside.

2. The salt will draw some of the liquid from the aubergines. After a few minutes, brush the slices with olive oil and season with pepper. Cook the aubergines on a hot griddle pan evenly on both sides.

3. While the aubergines are cooking, mix the feta, tomatoes, cucumber and parsley together with some salt and a squeeze of lemon.

4. When the aubergine slices are cooked, transfer to a serving plate and serve them hot with the feta mixture arranged on top.

Couscous & Bean Salad

*This colourful salad adds a burst of flavour
to any picnic or barbecue.*

INGREDIENTS

100g couscous
160ml vegetable stock or boiling water
2 sticks of celery, thinly sliced
6 chilli olives, sliced
6 chilli peppers, pickled and sliced
125g mixed beans, fresh or tinned

125g feta cheese, cubed
Juice of ½ lemon
2 tablespoons parsley, chopped
1 tablespoon mint, chopped
Salt and pepper, to taste
Seeds of ½ a pomegranate (optional)

METHOD

1. Soak the couscous in the stock or boiled water, leaving it to stand in a covered bowl for 8 to 10 minutes. When the water is fully absorbed, fluff the couscous and leave it to cool for 30 minutes.

2. When the couscous is cold, add the celery, chilli olives, chilli peppers, the mixed beans and feta cubes.

3. In a separate bowl combine the lemon juice, parsley and mint and season with salt and pepper. Pour over the couscous mixture and fold everything together.

4. To serve, mix in the pomegranate seeds.

Roasted Butternut Squash & Mixed Leaf Salad

This salad is hearty enough to enjoy as a main,
but light enough to be shared as a side or starter.

INGREDIENTS

½ a butternut squash, peeled and chopped into 1cm cubes

1 tablespoon olive oil

Salt and pepper, to taste

25g pine nuts

80g salad leaves (rocket, spinach and watercress)

1 medium avocado, diced into 1cm cubes

100g mozzarella balls or pearls

Balsamic vinegar glaze, for drizzling

METHOD

1. Preheat the oven to 200°C.

2. Toss the butternut squash cubes in the olive oil before seasoning with salt and pepper. Place the cubes on greaseproof paper and roast in a hot oven for 25 to 30 minutes until they are lightly browned.

3. Spread the pine nuts on a baking tray and toast them in the oven for 5 to 10 minutes until golden.

4. Place the salad leaves in a bowl, add the roasted butternut squash, chopped avocado, toasted pine nuts and the mozzarella.

5. Serve with a drizzle of balsamic glaze.

Mexican Vegetable Soup

A filling and hearty, hot and sour soup.

INGREDIENTS

5-6 fresh tomatoes

1 tablespoon vegetable oil

1 teaspoon cumin seeds

2 teaspoons salt

Red chilli powder or fresh green chillies, to taste

½ teaspoon turmeric powder

2 x 400g kidney beans, tinned

4-5 medium carrots, finely grated

1 medium courgette, finely grated

Handful of spinach (optional)

Handful of fresh coriander

6 cloves of garlic, crushed

2 small white onions, chopped

3 teaspoons sugar

Juice of ½ a lemon

METHOD

1. Begin by boiling the tomatoes until soft and then blending them in the food processor (you can put the mixture through a sieve after blending but it's not necessary).

2. Heat the oil in a pan and fry the cumin seeds. Add the tomatoes and bring to the boil.

3. Next add the salt, chilli and turmeric, then add the kidney beans and leave the mixture to boil for 5 minutes, until the kidney beans are soft and slightly mushy.

4. When the beans are cooked, add the carrots, courgette, spinach and coriander and leave to simmer on a low heat for 10 minutes.

5. Add the crushed garlic, chopped onions and the sugar and leave to simmer for 15 minutes.

6. Take the soup off the heat, finish with the juice of half a lemon and serve immediately.

Grilled Halloumi, Avocado & Mango Salad

*All the flavours of summer
in every refreshing mouthful*

INGREDIENTS

½ fresh mango

Mixed salad leaves

1 fresh mango, cubed

1 avocado, sliced thinly lengthways

250g halloumi cheese

200g honey roasted cashew nuts

Salt and pepper, to taste

METHOD

1. Begin by placing the half mango into a blender and pulp to a thick purée.

2. Add half of the mango purée to the salad leaves followed by the cubed mango and sliced avocado.

3. To grill the halloumi, slice it into 1cm thick pieces and fry in a pan until it turns golden, or alternatively cook in a panini grill, then add it to the salad.

4. Crush the roasted cashews and sprinkle them over the salad.

5. Lastly, season the salad with salt and pepper.

6. Serve immediately, with the remaining mango purée poured over the salad.

Sweet Potato & Chickpea Soup

A hearty soup, packed with natural goodness.

INGREDIENTS

3 tablespoons chilli-infused olive oil, plus extra to drizzle

1 large red onion, diced

2-3 cloves of garlic, minced

1-2 chillies, crushed (optional)

2 leeks, trimmed and chopped

500g frozen or fresh sweet potatoes, diced

3 teaspoons curry powder

Salt, to taste

900ml hot vegetable stock

420g chickpeas, rinsed and drained

125g halloumi cheese

4 tablespoons five seed mix or any seed mix of choice

2 tablespoons fresh flat-leaf parsley, chopped

METHOD

1. To start, heat two tablespoons of the chilli oil in a large saucepan. Gently fry the onion, garlic and chillies in the oil, until the onion starts browning. Next add the leeks and cook for 5 minutes until softened. Add the sweet potatoes and fry, stirring for a further 3 minutes.

2. Next, add the curry powder and salt to the potato mixture. Pour in the stock and bring to the boil. Then reduce the heat, cover and simmer gently. After 5 minutes, add the chickpeas into the pan and cook for a further 5 minutes.

3. While the potato mixture cooks, pat dry the halloumi on kitchen paper and slice into strips. Heat the remaining oil in a small frying pan and gently fry the halloumi for 1 minute, turning regularly. Add in the seed mix and continue to pan fry, stirring, for a further 1 to 2 minutes, or until the halloumi begins to colour.

4. Lastly, using an electric hand blender or potato masher, blend the soup until the vegetables are crushed but not fully puréed. Ladle the soup into bowls and scatter with the halloumi and seeds. To serve, sprinkle with the parsley and a drizzle of extra chilli oil and enjoy with a brown batch loaf.

Hearty Bean Salad

*A refreshing protein enriched salad
that leaves you feeling satisfied.*

INGREDIENTS

2 potatoes, cut into cubes

100g green beans, halved

400g black eyed beans, tinned

4 spring onions, finely chopped

1 fresh chilli, chopped

1 tomato, chopped

Handful of herbs

(any combination of coriander, parsley, mint)

1 mango, chopped

½ pomegranate

For the dressing

2 tablespoons olive oil or rapeseed oil

1 tablespoon lemon juice

1 teaspoon honey

Salt and pepper, to taste

METHOD

1. In separate pans, boil the potatoes and green beans until they are just cooked. Then combine these with all of the remaining salad ingredients in a large bowl.

2. To make the dressing, combine all the ingredients together and mix thoroughly.

3. To serve, pour the dressing over the salad.

Tip: You can add other vegetables such as sweetcorn or asparagus when in season.

Mexican Quinoa Salad

Happy healthy eating with an interesting combination of flavours.

INGREDIENTS

1 tablespoon olive oil

2 cloves of garlic, minced

1 jalapeño, minced

400g black beans, drained and rinsed

200g sweetcorn

1 teaspoon chilli powder or taco spice mix

½ teaspoon ground cumin

170g quinoa, cooked in 500ml of vegetable stock

55g sun-dried tomatoes

Salt and black pepper, to taste

1 avocado, halved, peeled and diced

Juice of 1 lime

2 tablespoons fresh coriander, chopped

METHOD

1. To start, heat the olive oil in a large pan over medium-high heat.

2. Add the garlic and jalapeño and fry for about a minute, stirring frequently, until fragrant.

3. Add the black beans, sweetcorn, chilli or taco spice mix and cumin.

4. Next, stir in the cooked quinoa and sun-dried tomatoes then season with salt and pepper, to taste.

5. Just before serving stir in the avocado and lime juice and top with chopped coriander.

South Indian Cucumber Salad

Hot, crunchy and cooling, all in one bite.

INGREDIENTS

1 full sized cucumber

2 red hot chillies

50g coriander, freshly chopped

1 tablespoon sunflower oil

1 teaspoon mustard seeds

10 curry leaves

1 teaspoon salt

3 teaspoons sugar

400g either honey roasted cashews or peanuts

15g desiccated coconut

METHOD

1. Quarter the cucumber lengthwise and then thinly slice each section.

2. Finely chop the chillies and the coriander leaves and mix with the cucumber.

3. Meanwhile, in a pan heat the oil then fry the mustard seeds and curry leaves. When the mixture starts to crackle, add this to the cucumber mixture and stir.

4. The mixture can then be left in the fridge for a few hours or overnight to allow the cucumber to take on the heat of the chillies.

5. When ready to serve season with salt and sugar, add the crushed nuts and coconut, then serve immediately.

Irio
(Kenyan Vegetable Mash)

Healthy, comforting and perfect after a heavy weekend.

INGREDIENTS

1 large white potato
1 large carrot, grated
100g peas
100g sweetcorn
300g kidney beans
1 onion, chopped

Fresh green chilli, to taste
1 teaspoon fresh ginger, minced
6 cubes of frozen spinach
Lemon juice, to taste
Salt and pepper, to taste

METHOD

1. Steam the potato, carrot, peas and sweetcorn until tender.

2. Boil the kidney beans in a saucepan, retaining the cooking water. Mash all the steamed vegetables and beans together.

3. Fry the onion, chilli and ginger for 5 minutes or until soft, add the spinach and cook for a further 4 to 5 minutes. Next, add the mashed vegetables and some of the water from the kidney beans.

4. Season the mixture with the salt, pepper and lemon juice.

5. Serve with bread rolls.

Italian Bean & Olive Salad

*The perfect Mediterranean salad
to accompany any barbecue.*

INGREDIENTS

2 yellow bell peppers, halved

2 red bell peppers, halved

300g green beans

300g cherry tomatoes, halved

1 tablespoon small capers

2 handfuls of black olives, stoned

4 tablespoons olive oil

1 tablespoon red wine vinegar

Large bunch of basil, roughly shredded

Balsamic glaze

METHOD

1. In a grill pan or over a flame, roast the peppers, place in a bowl and cover with cling film. Once cool, peel, deseed and cut into strips, keeping any of the juices.

2. In salted water, boil the green beans until cooked but still crunchy.

3. Toss the peppers, beans and all of the other ingredients together, except the basil and balsamic glaze.

4. Add the shredded basil just before serving and drizzle the balsamic glaze over the salad.

Leek & Sweetcorn Soup

A lighter version of the classic Chinese soup.

INGREDIENTS

150g baby leeks

3 sticks of celery

Fresh green chilli, to taste

1 tablespoon olive oil

375g creamed style sweetcorn

1 vegetable stock cube

500ml water

Salt and pepper, to taste

Fresh red and green chilli, to garnish

METHOD

1. Start by finely chopping the leeks and the celery.

2. Gently fry the leeks, celery and chilli in oil, allowing them to soften.

3. When the vegetables are soft add the tin of corn, a stock cube and 500ml of water.

4. Simmer for 10 minutes and season to taste.

5. Garnish with fresh chilli and serve with warm crusty bread.

peckish
delicious food doesn't have to take an age

Quinoa Veggie Bowls

Bowls of goodness with big, bold Asian flavours.

INGREDIENTS

1 tablespoon vegetable oil

120g tenderstem broccoli tips, halved lengthways

1 red bell pepper, cut into chunks

160g marinated tofu pieces

185g quinoa, cooked

150g edamame beans

1 tablespoon sesame seeds

3 spring onions, chopped

For the sauce

1 red chilli, deseeded and finely chopped

1 clove of garlic, crushed

1 inch piece fresh ginger, grated

3 tablespoons soy sauce

1 tablespoon sweet chilli sauce

1 tablespoon rice wine vinegar

Salt, to taste

METHOD

1. For the sauce, mix the chilli, garlic, ginger, soy, sweet chilli sauce and vinegar in a bowl. Set aside.

2. Heat the oil in a wok, add the broccoli and pepper then stir fry over a high heat for about 3 minutes. Add the tofu, cook for another 1 to 2 minutes until crisp. Add the cooked quinoa and stir fry for 4 minutes, breaking up the grains as they warm through. Add the edamame beans and cook for a further 2 to 3 minutes. Finally, pour the sauce over the quinoa mixture and toss until coated and warmed through.

3. To serve, spoon into bowls and scatter over the sesame seeds and spring onions.

Spinach, Mushroom & Feta Parcels

Greek-inspired pastry parcels.

INGREDIENTS

2 tablespoons rapeseed oil

1 onion, finely chopped

250g chestnut mushrooms, sliced

500g spinach, chopped

2-3 tablespoons dill, finely chopped

Salt and pepper, to taste

250g feta cheese, chopped

320g ready-rolled puff pastry, at room temperature

1 egg, beaten

2 tablespoons sesame seeds, for sprinkling

METHOD

1. Preheat the oven to 200°C.

2. Heat the oil and fry the onion until it's golden brown. Add the mushrooms and spinach then stir fry until the natural juices have evaporated. Season to taste with salt and pepper.

3. Add the dill, cook the mixture for about 5 to 7 minutes and then remove from the heat.

4. Add the feta and leave the mixture to cool.

5. Cut the pastry sheets into ten squares. When the mixture is cool, place a spoonful of the mixture on one half of each pastry square, making sure to leave at least a centimetre around the edge. Fold over the other half of the pastry square and brush the edges of each parcel with the beaten egg to seal.

6. Glaze with beaten egg then sprinkle with sesame seeds and place in a hot oven for 15 minutes or until golden brown.

7. Serve hot with your favourite accompaniment.

Tortilla Con Funghi

A delicious starter or a light lunch.

INGREDIENTS

1 tablespoon olive oil

1 red onion, sliced

2 cloves of garlic, chopped

300g chestnut mushrooms, sliced

200ml single light cream

A handful of flat leaf parsley, chopped

Salt and pepper, for seasoning

3 tortilla wraps

Balsamic glaze, for drizzling

METHOD

1. Heat the oil in a pan. Add the onion and garlic and fry for about 2 minutes on a low heat.

2. Add in the mushrooms and cook until they are soft and letting out their natural juices. Allow any moisture to evaporate and then add the cream.

3. Leave the mixture to simmer on a medium heat for about 3-4 minutes, then add the parsley, setting a little aside for serving, and continue cooking until the sauce becomes quite thick. Season to taste with salt and pepper.

4. Meanwhile, cut the tortillas into quarters and toast them under the grill until they are brown and crisp. Top each tortilla with some of the mushroom mixture and serve with a sprinkling of parsley and a drizzle of balsamic glaze.

Khandvi (Tempered Chickpea Rolls)

The tempered spices bring to life these simple gram flour rolls.

INGREDIENTS

150g gram flour
900ml water, at room temperature
½ teaspoon turmeric
1 teaspoon salt

For tempering
1 tablespoon oil
1 green chilli (optional)
1 teaspoon mustard seeds
3 teaspoons sesame seeds
2 tablespoons desiccated coconut
Handful fresh coriander leaves, finely chopped

METHOD

1. Whisk the gram flour, water, turmeric and salt together. Heat a pan and add the gram flour mixture, stirring consistently on a medium heat.

2. After about 20 minutes of continuous stirring, the mixture should thicken and create 'sink holes' in the pan. To test whether the mixture is ready, spread a small amount thinly on a plate and allow it to cool for about 30 seconds. If the mixture peels away from the plate smoothly without residue, it is ready.

3. Remove the mixture from the heat and spread it thinly on a clean surface, creating a large rectangle. Allow the mixture to cool for 5 minutes and then using a knife, draw vertical lines about 10cm apart across the width of the rectangle. Then using your hands, roll up each vertical strip of the mixture like a Swiss roll and cut each roll into two or three smaller rolls.

4. In a small frying pan, heat the oil and fry the green chilli, mustard seeds and sesame seeds until the sesame seeds turn golden. Sprinkle the toasted seeds over the gram flour rolls.

5. To serve, sprinkle with desiccated coconut and chopped coriander.

PECKISH
makes eight to ten
preparation time: 20 minutes ❖ cooking time: 40 minutes

Pinwheel Samosas

*A fun twist on the classic Indian samosa,
perfect served with masala chai.*

INGREDIENTS

3-4 large white potatoes, boiled
110g peas
1 carrot, grated (optional)
Salt, to taste
2 teaspoons mango powder
2 teaspoons cumin powder
2 teaspoons cornflour

1 tablespoon sunflower oil
1 medium onion, finely chopped
1-2 green chillies to taste, finely chopped
320g ready-rolled puff pastry, at room temperature
100g coriander chutney (see page 142)
Milk, for glazing
Melted butter, for glazing (optional)

METHOD

1. Preheat the oven to 200°C.

2. Mash the boiled potatoes then add the peas, carrot, salt, mango powder, cumin powder and cornflour. Heat the oil in a pan and gently fry the onion and chillies until the onion is soft and transparent. Add this to the potato mixture and mix well.

3. Roll out the pastry, and spread the coriander chutney all over the pastry leaving a small border around the edge. Spread the potato mixture on to the pastry, over the chutney. Roll the pastry with the potato mixture so you have what looks like a Swiss roll.

4. Brush the exposed edge with milk to seal, making sure the end of the roll sticks firmly in place. Cut the roll into slices about half an inch thick.

5. Place the rounds on a baking tray lined with baking paper and lightly brush with milk or melted butter to glaze. Bake for 20 to 25 minutes, or until golden brown. Serve hot with coriander chutney or tomato ketchup.

Rava Uttapams (Savoury Vegetable Pancakes)

Low fat savoury pancakes packed full of vegetables.

INGREDIENTS

240g yoghurt
170g medium coarse semolina
1 teaspoon salt
1 red potato, grated
1 carrot, grated
1 red bell pepper, chopped
1 red onion, chopped
2 tablespoons fresh coriander, chopped

2 green chillies
¼ teaspoon baking powder
For tempering
2 tablespoons vegetable oil
1 teaspoon mustard seeds
1 teaspoon cumin seeds
4 curry leaves

METHOD

1. Mix the yoghurt and the semolina so it creates a smooth paste. Then add the salt, potato, carrot, pepper, onion, chillies and coriander to the paste. Loosen the batter with up to 235ml of water so it ends up slightly thicker than pancake batter.

2. In a frying pan, heat the vegetable oil and fry the mustard seeds, cumin seeds and curry leaves until they 'pop'. Immediately add these ingredients to the batter followed by the baking powder.

3. With a ladle, pour the mixture into a greased frying pan, so each pancake is about 1cm thick. Fry the pancake on both sides until golden.

4. Serve with coconut chutney (see page 143).

Minty Summer Rolls

Colourful rice paper rolls full of summer flavours.

INGREDIENTS

For the rolls
25g rice vermicelli noodles
¼ cucumber, deseeded and julienned
1 red bell pepper, deseeded and julienned
100g red cabbage, shredded
A handful of fresh mint leaves
A handful of coriander, leaves picked
8 rice paper wraps

For the dressing
½ tablespoon rice vinegar
½ teaspoon sugar
1 teaspoon soy sauce
½ lime, juiced
Chilli flakes, to taste

METHOD

1. For the rolls, place the noodles into a heatproof bowl, and cover them with boiling water. Set them aside for 5 minutes and leave to soften. When they are done, drain the noodles, add the vegetables and herbs to the noodles and set them aside.

2. Fill a shallow dish with warm water and submerge each rice paper wrap in the water for one minute to soften it. Remove the rice paper from the water and place on a chopping board. Arrange some of the noodle mixture in the centre of each paper. Be careful not to put too much on or it will be too thick to roll.

3. Fold in the sides of each piece of rice paper and then roll them up tightly to make neat parcels.

4. For the dressing, whisk together the rice vinegar, sugar, soy sauce, lime juice and chilli flakes in a bowl. Serve the summer rolls with the dressing.

Tip: You can make these using white cabbage, tofu or bean sprouts, or choose your favourite veggies.

Paniyaram (Rice & Lentil Puffed Dumplings)

*Tasty little rice balls with a savoury filling
that make a delicious snack.*

INGREDIENTS

2 tablespoons green coriander chutney (see page 142)

85g sweetcorn

60g cheddar cheese, grated

1 spring onion, finely chopped (optional)

480g dosa batter (a ready-made rice and lentil batter that is available from any Indian grocery store)

METHOD

1. First, mix the green chutney, sweetcorn, cheese and spring onion together.

2. Heat a well-greased 'Appe' or 'Paniyaram' pan and fill each mould about half full with dosa batter.

3. Add a teaspoon of the chutney mixture, on top of the batter in each mould. Top up with more dosa batter so that the chutney mixture sits in the middle.

4. Cover the pan with a lid and cook on a medium heat for about 5 minutes until each ball is brown on one side, then flip them and cook for a further 2 to 3 minutes until golden brown.

5. Once cooked, remove the balls from the pan and serve hot with your chutney of choice.

Stuffed Mushrooms

*Earthy mushrooms bursting with
the rich flavours of Emmental and cheddar.*

INGREDIENTS

500g mushrooms (cup or chestnut)

1 tablespoon olive oil

4 cloves of garlic, minced

1 green or red chilli to taste, seeds removed and finely chopped

85g soft cream cheese

100g Emmental cheese, grated

50g cheddar, grated

1 lemon, juiced

30g golden breadcrumbs

4 tablespoon chopped fresh coriander

5 tablespoon chopped fresh chives

Sea salt and freshly ground black pepper, to taste

METHOD

1. Preheat the oven to 180°C. Grease a baking dish.

2. Carefully remove the stems from the mushrooms and chop the stems finely. Heat the olive oil in a frying pan and sauté the chopped mushroom stems with the garlic and chilli until softened and the mushrooms release moisture. This should take about 5 minutes.

3. In a small bowl, combine the cream cheese with half of the Emmental and all the cheddar. Stir in the cooked mushroom mixture, lemon juice, 20g of the breadcrumbs, coriander and chives. Season to taste with salt and pepper.

4. Spoon the mixture into the mushroom cups, so that it slightly overfills the mushrooms. Top with the remaining golden breadcrumbs and grated Emmental.

5. Place the stuffed mushrooms in the prepared baking dish and bake in the oven for 15 to 20 minutes, or until the cheese begins to brown. Serve immediately.

Open Grilled Vegetable Sandwich

A sandwich with substance.

INGREDIENTS

For the filling

2 carrots, grated

1 large tomato, deseeded and finely chopped

1 red onion, finely chopped

1 green chilli, finely chopped (optional)

250g cheddar cheese, grated

25g coriander, finely chopped

2 teaspoons West Indian pepper sauce (or to taste)

Salt, to taste

For the bread

1 French bread stick, cut in 4 inch pieces
then halved horizontally

Butter for the bread

METHOD

1. Mix all of the ingredients for the filling together.

2. Butter the flat side of the bread and spread the filling mixture on the buttered side.

3. Place the baguettes in a baking tray under a hot grill until the cheese melts and bubbles.

4. Serve hot with tomato ketchup.

Sesame & Peanut Noodles

A great and versatile oriental noodle salad with a perfect balance of Asian flavours.

INGREDIENTS

For the dressing
4 tablespoons lime juice
4 tablespoons chilli sauce
2 tablespoons sesame oil
2 tablespoons garlic infused oil
2 tablespoons soy sauce
2 tablespoons peanut butter
(All the above measurements can be adjusted according to your personal taste)

For the noodles
1 tablespoon sesame seeds
300g bean sprouts
75g mangetout, thinly sliced
1 red bell pepper, thinly sliced
1 yellow bell pepper, thinly sliced
300g fresh egg noodles
4 spring onions, thinly sliced
1 tablespoon rapeseed oil
Fresh coriander, finely chopped

METHOD

1. For the dressing, place all the ingredients into a bowl and mix well. Set aside.

2. In a frying pan heat the sesame seeds on a very low flame for a few minutes until they have browned. Set these aside until ready to serve.

3. Mix together the bean sprouts, mangetout and the red and yellow peppers in a salad bowl and set aside.

4. In a hot wok, heat the oil and add the noodles to warm through thoroughly. Once cooked, add the noodles to the salad bowl. Pour over the dressing and stir well. To serve, sprinkle over the toasted sesame seeds, spring onions and chopped coriander.

Tip: This dish doesn't have to be served hot, room temperature is absolutely fine.

PECKISH
serves two to three
preparation time: 10 minutes ❖ cooking time: 20 minutes

Tortellini & Tomato Soup

A meal in a soup with a slight kick

INGREDIENTS

2 teaspoons olive oil
1 medium onion, chopped
3 cloves of garlic, minced
1½ teaspoons dried Italian seasoning
½ teaspoon red chilli flakes, crushed
½ teaspoon salt

¼ teaspoon coarsely ground black pepper
750ml vegetable stock
400g chopped tomatoes
1 packet of cheese and spinach tortellini
2 large handfuls of baby spinach

METHOD

1. Heat the oil in a large pot and fry the onion, garlic, Italian seasoning, chilli flakes, salt and pepper over a medium heat for about 4 minutes until the onion is tender.

2. Stir in the vegetable stock and tomatoes and bring the mixture to the boil.

3. Add the tortellini and cook for another few minutes until it's cooked through.

4. Lastly, add the baby spinach and allow it to wilt slightly.

5. Serve hot with crusty bread.

Paneer Tikka

*Using tikka spices to create
an exciting vegetarian option.*

INGREDIENTS

225g paneer
1 red bell pepper
1 red onion
1 tablespoon olive oil
1 tablespoon water

½ tablespoon garlic, minced
½ tablespoon ginger, minced
1½ tablespoons natural yoghurt
1 tablespoon tandoori masala powder
Salt, to taste

METHOD

1. Cut the paneer into 12 big cubed pieces and then cut the pepper and onion into similar sized pieces. Next put the olive oil, water, garlic, ginger, yoghurt, tandoori masala powder and a pinch of salt into a bowl. Add the paneer, red pepper and onion pieces into the mixture, ensuring they are completely covered in the marinade. Leave to marinate overnight.

2. When the paneer is marinated, heat the oven to 200°C, then lay the paneer, pepper and onion pieces on a baking tray and bake for 15 to 20 minutes until they are lightly charred. Turn once halfway through.

3. Can be served either on its own or in a warmed pitta with salad.

Share
food to enjoy
with friends

Warm Parmesan & Artichoke Dip

*This dip is an absolute must for parties.
Oozy, rich and so moreish you won't have any left.*

INGREDIENTS

400g artichoke hearts, tinned,
drained and chopped
240g mayonnaise

125g Parmesan cheese, grated
1 clove of garlic, crushed (optional)
Chilli flakes (optional)

METHOD

1. Preheat the oven to 180°C.

2. Start by mixing the artichoke hearts, the mayonnaise and 100g of the Parmesan cheese in a bowl. Add the garlic if desired and the chilli flakes to taste.

3. Next, pour the mixture into an ovenproof dish.

4. Finish by sprinkling the remaining Parmesan cheese on top.

5. Bake in a preheated oven for 20 minutes until the top turns brown.

6. Serve immediately with warm bread or crackers.

Smoked Aubergine Crostini

A Lebanese spiced spread that can be prepared in advance and served on a crostini as a canapé.

INGREDIENTS

2 aubergines
1 tablespoon rapeseed oil
2 teaspoons sesame oil
1 tablespoon tahini
1 lemon, juiced
2 teaspoons baharat spice

½ green chilli, chopped
2 tablespoons parsley, chopped
Salt, to taste
2 tablespoons sesame seeds, toasted
½ pomegranate, seeds only
1 seeded baguette, sliced

METHOD

1. Prick the aubergines with a fork and brush them with rapeseed oil before grilling them for 30 minutes until the skin is charred and the flesh soft.

2. Remove them from the heat, peel off the blackened skins and mash the flesh with a fork.

3. In a bowl combine the mashed aubergines with the sesame oil, tahini, lemon juice, baharat, parsley, chilli and salt.

4. To serve, spread the aubergine mixture on slices of toasted baguette, or your favourite bread and finish with a sprinkling of pomegranate and sesame seeds.

Feta & Mint Bites

*These can be served as canapés
or as the star of a main dish.*

INGREDIENTS

200g feta cheese
Handful of fresh mint
2 teaspoons nigella seeds

320g ready-rolled puff pastry, at room temperature
A little milk or 1 egg, beaten

METHOD

1. Preheat the oven to 190°C.

2. Crumble the feta into a bowl and mix in the mint and nigella seeds.

3. Next, roll out the puff pastry and cut into eight equal squares.

4. Place the feta mixture on one half of the square pastry sheet and fold over opposite corners. Press the edges together with a fork. Make sure you seal the parcel well otherwise it will open up when cooking.

5. Glaze the pastry with milk or a beaten egg, before placing in the oven for 20 minutes until golden brown and cooked through.

6. Serve immediately.

Oven-Roasted Spiced Broccoli

Simply adding some Indian spices can bring your
roasted vegetables to life.

INGREDIENTS

2 large heads of broccoli, cut into florets

2 tablespoons olive oil

1½ teaspoons mango powder

1 teaspoon chaat masala

½ teaspoon red chilli powder

Pinch of salt

METHOD

1. Preheat the oven to 160°C.

2. Arrange the broccoli florets on a baking tray. Drizzle over the oil and mix thoroughly to ensure they are evenly covered.

3. Roast the broccoli in the middle of the hot oven for about 30 to 35 minutes.

4. Combine the mango powder, chaat masala, red chilli powder and salt to make the spice mixture. The spices can be adjusted according to your taste.

5. When the broccoli begins to char slightly around the edges, remove the tray from the oven and sprinkle the spice mix over the broccoli, stirring thoroughly so it's evenly covered.

6. Return the broccoli to the oven for a further 10 minutes and serve immediately.

Potato & Sweetcorn Ondhwo

An alternative to a classic Gujarati dish

INGREDIENTS

3 medium red-skinned potatoes

3 medium white-skinned potatoes

3 slices of bread

Splash of milk

200g sweetcorn

1-2 teaspoons salt

½ teaspoon turmeric

¾ teaspoon red chilli powder

1 teaspoon green chilli, crushed

1 teaspoon ginger, crushed

Pinch of sugar

Juice of ½ a lemon or lime

A handful of coriander, chopped

½ teaspoon mustard seeds

2 small cinnamon sticks

A handful of cashews

A few curry leaves

1 tablespoon sesame seeds

2 tablespoons rapeseed oil

METHOD

1. Preheat the oven to 180°C. Boil the potatoes and then remove the skin, before mashing them thoroughly. In a separate dish, soak each slice of bread in some milk, gently squeeze out the excess and add the bread to the potatoes along with the sweetcorn. Add the salt, turmeric, chilli, ginger, sugar, lemon juice and coriander and mix thoroughly. Taste the mixture and add more seasoning if required, then set aside.

2. Heat a tablespoon of rapeseed oil in a pan and fry the mustard seeds to temper until they start to splutter slightly, then add the cinnamon, cashews and curry leaves. Leave this to cook for a minute, turn off the heat and add the oil and its contents to the potato mixture, stirring it through. Put the mixture into an 8-inch baking dish and spread the mixture out evenly.

3. Sprinkle the bake with sesame seeds. Heat the other tablespoon of oil and when warm, pour this over the sesame seeds.

4. Put the bake in the oven for about 30 to 40 minutes, until the top has browned slightly.

5. Allow to cool a little before cutting into slices to serve.

Fruit & Nut Camembert

A must for cheese lovers.

INGREDIENTS

2 x 250g Camembert

250g apricot jam, at room temperature

1 fresh green chilli, chopped

1 fresh red chilli, chopped

150g roasted nuts, roughly chopped

40g apricots, sliced (optional)

1 stick French bread, thinly sliced

Olive oil, for brushing bread

METHOD

1. Preheat the oven to 180°C.

2. Place one Camembert on a baking tray covered with baking paper. Spread the Camembert generously with half the jam and sprinkle on half of the chillies, nuts and apricots if using.

3. Take the other Camembert and place it on top of the first before repeating the process with the remaining ingredients. Then arrange the slices of bread around the baking tray and brush them with olive oil.

4. Bake in a hot oven for 12 to 15 minutes until the cheese is soft and just beginning to melt.

5. Serve immediately with the toasted bread.

Khow Suey

A Burmese dish with a delicately spiced coconut sauce and noodles.

INGREDIENTS

250g spaghetti or noodles

For the chilli garlic oil

4-5 cloves of garlic, sliced

120ml sunflower oil

1 heaped teaspoon red chilli powder

For the coconut sauce

2 tablespoons gram flour

120g plain yoghurt

400g coconut milk, tinned

400ml water

7-8 curry leaves

2 green chillies, sliced

1 inch fresh ginger, finely sliced

300g boiled mixed vegetables,

Salt, to taste

For the toppings

Potato matchstick crisps or sev

Coriander, chopped

Lemon, cut into wedges

Onions or spring onions, chopped

Chilli flakes or fresh green chilli, chopped

Salted peanuts, roughly crushed

METHOD

1. For the chilli garlic oil, heat the oil in a small pan, then fry the garlic in the hot oil until it browns. Carefully pour the cooked garlic and oil in a bowl to cool. Once cool, add the chilli powder and cover.

2. For the coconut sauce, add the yoghurt and gram flour to a bowl, mix well to make a smooth paste and set aside. In a large pan mix the coconut milk and water. Add the yoghurt paste and blend well. Heat the sauce on a medium heat. Add the curry leaves, green chillies and ginger. Bring this sauce to the boil, then turn down the heat and let the mixture simmer for about 30 minutes. Next add the mixed vegetables and salt, and simmer for a further 15 minutes.

3. Boil the spaghetti or noodles according to the packet instructions.

4. Place the noodles in a bowl and cover generously with the coconut sauce. To this add some chilli garlic oil and a little bit of each of the toppings. Customise the dish to your individual taste.

Baked Ragda Pattis

A healthy version of the traditional Indian street food.

INGREDIENTS

For the Ragda curry
300g dry white peas, soaked
overnight
2 tablespoons oil
¼ teaspoon asafoetida
2-3 cloves
2 x 1 inch cinnamon sticks
½ teaspoon turmeric
1 teaspoon red chilli powder
2 teaspoons ground
coriander-cumin powder
2 tablespoons lemon juice
1-2 teaspoons sugar
Salt, to taste

For the green pea mixture
450g frozen peas, defrosted
1 tablespoon oil
¼ teaspoon asafoetida
½ teaspoon mustard seeds
¼ teaspoon turmeric
1½ teaspoons garam masala
1-2 teaspoons sugar
2 tablespoons lemon juice
1 teaspoon ginger chilli paste
Salt, to taste
50g coconut, shredded
Handful of coriander, roughly
chopped

For the potato mixture
1kg potatoes
1 tablespoon cornflour
Salt, to taste
Toppings
Green chutney (see page 142)
Tamarind & date chutney
(see page 143)
Red onion, chopped
Coriander leaves
Sev

METHOD

1. For the Ragda curry, drain the white peas and boil until soft. Heat the oil in a pan and add the asafoetida, cloves and cinnamon followed by the cooked white peas and all the other ingredients for the curry. Simmer for 10 minutes until the curry is blended. The consistency should be that of thick gravy. Add a little water if the mixture is too thick.

2. For the potato mixture, peel, boil and mash the potatoes, add the cornflour and salt.

3. For the green pea mixture, roughly mash the peas. Heat the oil in a pan, add the asafoetida, mustard seeds, the mashed peas and all the remaining spices, sugar, lemon juice and chilli paste. Cook on a low heat for 5 minutes, remove from heat and once cooled, add the shredded coconut and coriander.

4. Preheat the oven to 200°C. To assemble the recipe, grease an ovenproof dish and add half of the potato mixture at the bottom in an even layer. Next add the green pea mixture. Follow this with the remaining potato mixture. Lightly brush with oil and bake in the oven for 30 to 40 minutes until golden brown.

5. To serve, place a piece of the potato and pea bake into a bowl and add a generous portion of the Radga curry. Add all of the toppings to your liking. You can serve with green chutney, sev, tamarind and date chutney, chopped onion and a sprinkling of coriander leaves and enjoy while hot.

Patra Chaat

An unusual way of turning the humble patra into a delicious Indian street food.

INGREDIENTS

12 frozen patra pieces (available in Indian stores)

For tempering

1 tablespoon oil

½ teaspoon mustard seeds

4-5 curry leaves

1 teaspoon sesame seeds

For the potato and tomato mixture

1 tablespoon oil

1 teaspoon cumin seeds

3 tomatoes, deseeded and diced

2 large potatoes, diced

Salt, to taste

1 teaspoon red chilli powder, to taste

For the yoghurt

300g plain yoghurt

2 teaspoons chaat masala

Salt, to taste

For the toppings

1 onion, finely chopped

3-4 tablespoons green coriander chutney (see page 142)

3-4 tablespoons tamarind chutney (see page 143)

Sev, to garnish

Coriander, to garnish

METHOD

1. For the patra, heat the oil in a pan, add the mustard seeds, curry leaves and sesame seeds. When the spices begin to sizzle add the sliced patra and set aside.

2. For the potato and tomato mixture, heat the oil in a pan, add the cumin seeds, when they begin to sizzle add the tomatoes and cook for a couple of minutes. Add the potatoes, salt and red chilli powder, (add a small amount of water to help cook the potatoes if required). Cover and allow to simmer until the potatoes are cooked through. Once finished take it off the heat and set aside.

3. For the spiced yoghurt, beat the yoghurt until smooth, then season with salt and chaat masala.

4. Line a serving dish with the patra pieces. Add a generous layer of the tomato and potato mixture. Follow this by pouring over the spiced yoghurt and finish with a sprinkling of sev, onion, green chutney and tamarind chutney. Garnish with coriander and serve.

Oven-Baked Cheese & Broccoli Dip

Great for an extra warm welcome at parties.

INGREDIENTS

175g broccoli, chopped
½ onion, chopped
½ red bell pepper, chopped
25g Parmesan, grated
1 clove of garlic

110g cheddar cheese
4 tablespoons half fat crème fraîche or sour cream
4 tablespoons mayonnaise
Pepper, to taste

METHOD

1. Preheat the oven to 200°C.

2. Mix all of the ingredients together thoroughly and then transfer the mixture into a baking dish, or for a heartier version place in a crusty cob. Cover and cook for about 25 minutes.

3. When cooked, serve with hot pitta chips, or if you cooked the mixture in a cob, tear, dip and share.

SHARE
serves four to six
preparation time: 45 minutes ❖ *cooking time: 30 minutes*

Aubergine & Pea Rolls

So impressive, so quick, so healthy.

INGREDIENTS

3 large Dutch aubergines
½ teaspoon salt
1 tablespoon sunflower oil
2 teaspoons ginger chilli paste (1 inch of fresh ginger
and two green chillies)
100g petit pois

1½ teaspoons sugar
½ lemon, juiced
1 teaspoon garam masala
2 tablespoons desiccated coconut
Oil for brushing

METHOD

1. Preheat the oven to 240°C.

2. Start by chopping the ends off the aubergines and cutting them lengthwise into slices about 1½cm thick. Sprinkle the slices with salt and leave for about 30 minutes, then pat dry to remove any excess liquid.

3. Meanwhile, heat a tablespoon of oil in a pan and fry the ginger chilli paste. Add the peas and cook for a few minutes, roughly mashing the peas as you cook. Season with salt and sugar, then add the lemon juice. Take the mixture off the heat, add the garam masala and leave the mixture to cool. Once cooled, mix the desiccated coconut into the peas mixture.

4. Lastly, brush the aubergines with oil and put them in the oven for 10 minutes on each side. Alternatively you can griddle them in a panini grill.

5. To assemble the dish, put a teaspoon of the pea mixture in the centre of each cooked aubergine slice and roll it up securing it with a cocktail stick, serve immediately.

Comfort

warm & welcoming dishes

COMFORT
serves six to eight
preparation time: 20 minutes ❖ *cooking time: 45 minutes*

Lemon Infused Rice with Raita

*A delicate citrus rice dish that can be eaten
with or without a curry.*

INGREDIENTS

For the lemon rice
300g basmati rice
Salt, to taste
1½ fresh lemons, juiced
1 tablespoon oil
20g split black lentils (urad dal), dehusked
1 teaspoon mustard seeds
A few curry leaves
Small bunch of coriander, chopped

For the raita
Small bunch of coriander
1 or 2 green chillies
1 clove of garlic (optional)
Salt, to taste
480g natural yoghurt

METHOD

1. Cook the rice in boiling water with salt and the rind of one lemon. Once the rice is cooked, set it aside.

2. In a separate pan, heat the oil and cook the urad dal until it starts to brown a little. Add the mustard seeds, curry leaves and a little salt, take it off the heat and add the lemon juice. Stir the oil mixture into the rice so the flavours are well incorporated. Taste the rice and add more salt and lemon as required.

3. For the raita, place the coriander, chillies, garlic and salt in a blender and blitz for 1 minute. Stir the mixture into the yoghurt so it is evenly distributed.

4. Serve the rice with the raita and an extra sprinkling of coriander.

COMFORT
serves four to six
preparation time: 15 minutes ❖ *cooking time: 15 minutes*

Tortilla Salad Bowls

Simple and nutritious, layer up to your taste.

INGREDIENTS

6 corn or wheat tortillas
½ head of lettuce, chopped
2 x 400g tins black beans, rinsed, drained and heated
2-3 tomatoes, diced
1 red onion, chopped
200g sweetcorn, tinned
Jalapeños to taste, chopped

1 yellow bell pepper, diced
1 red bell pepper, diced
200g cheddar cheese, grated
Handful of coriander, chopped
1 tablespoon taco mix
Fresh lemon juice, to taste

METHOD

1. Preheat the oven to 180°C.

2. Place each tortilla into an ovenproof bowl (you can buy special moulds for the tortillas but if you do not have these then an ovenproof bowl will do) and bake for 15 minutes or until golden brown, then set aside to cool.

3. To the black beans add the taco mix, coriander and lemon juice then mix thoroughly.

4. When cooled, fill the tortillas with the lettuce, black beans, tomatoes, onion, sweetcorn, peppers and jalapeños.

5. To finish, sprinkle with more coriander and grated cheese.

6. Serve the salad with Mexican dips such as salsa, sour cream and guacamole.

Quinoa Stuffed Roasted Peppers

Perfect for a low carb dinner.

INGREDIENTS

4 large red, yellow or orange bell peppers

170g quinoa

1 vegetable stock cube

400g black beans, drained

200g sweetcorn, drained

2 teaspoons ground cumin

1½ teaspoons chilli powder

1 clove of garlic, crushed

Salt and pepper, to taste

Tomato sauce, homemade or shop bought

100g cheddar cheese, grated

METHOD

1. Remove the top, keeping the stalk intact and deseed the peppers. Blanch them in boiling water for 2 minutes per pepper and then drain on a paper towel. Cook the quinoa according to the packet, using the vegetable stock cube.

2. In a large mixing bowl combine the cooked quinoa, black beans, sweetcorn, cumin, chilli and the garlic and then season with salt and pepper.

3. Season the inside of the peppers before stuffing them with the quinoa mixture.

4. Pour the tomato sauce into a large deep tray and arrange the peppers on top.

5. Sprinkle cheddar cheese on top and bake uncovered in the oven for 30 minutes.

Cashew Nut Curry with Halloumi & Broccoli

*A must for any halloumi lover; creamy,
gently-spiced and great to share.*

INGREDIENTS

2 tablespoons butter or oil

250g halloumi, cubed

400g coconut milk, tinned

135g cashews

500g passata

60g Greek yoghurt

1 white onion, diced

1-2 crushed chillies (optional)

3 cloves of garlic, minced

1½ inch piece ginger, grated

3 teaspoons curry powder

½ teaspoon garam masala

½ teaspoon turmeric

Salt, to taste

1 head broccoli, cut into florets and cooked

2 tablespoons fresh coriander, chopped

METHOD

1. Melt half of the butter in a saucepan. Fry the halloumi in the butter until it is browned on all sides. Place the halloumi on a plate covered with paper towels to drain.

2. Blend the coconut milk and 115g of the cashew nuts in a food processor until smooth. Then, add the passata and the yoghurt and blend again, adding a little water if the mixture needs loosening.

3. Melt the rest of the butter in a big pot before adding the onion, chillies, garlic, ginger and the rest of the cashew nuts. Stir fry for about 5 minutes, until all the ingredients have softened.

4. Add all the spices and the salt and fry for about 1 minute. When the mixture is fragrant, pour in the cashew nut mixture and bring to the boil. Then add the halloumi and broccoli to the sauce and cook for another 5 minutes. Serve hot with naan bread or rice and a sprinkling of coriander.

COMFORT
serves four to five
preparation time: 20 minutes ❖ *cooking time: 1 hour 10 minutes*

Vegetable Lasagne

Bursting with colourful vegetables.

INGREDIENTS

For the vegetable sauce
2 tablespoons rapeseed oil
250g chestnut mushrooms, chopped
260g spinach
2 large bell peppers (red and yellow)
2 large courgettes
1 onion, finely chopped
1 green chilli, finely chopped
325g passata
1 packet of lasagne seasoning mix
Salt and pepper, to taste

For the cheese sauce
50g butter
50g plain flour
500ml semi-skimmed milk
1 teaspoon English mustard
75g cheddar cheese, grated
Salt and pepper, to taste

For the lasagne
6-8 fresh lasagne sheets
25g Parmesan, grated
75g cheddar cheese, grated

METHOD

1. Preheat the oven to 190°C.

2. For the vegetable sauce, heat half a tablespoon of oil and lightly fry the mushrooms. Set aside. Steam the spinach, roughly chop it and set it aside. Cook the peppers and courgettes in a tablespoon of oil until they are slightly softened then set aside. Fry the onion in the rest of the oil until light brown. Add the passata and chilli and simmer for 10 minutes. Add the seasoning mix and the cooked mushrooms, peppers, spinach and courgettes. Season to taste with salt and pepper. Stir the sauce and then leave it to simmer for a further 15 minutes.

3. To make the cheese sauce, melt the butter on a low heat, then add the flour. Stir continuously until smooth and golden brown. Then begin slowly adding the milk, still mixing constantly. Wait for the sauce to thicken but try not to let it get too hot or stick to the bottom of the pan. When the sauce thickens, add the mustard and the cheese and season with salt and pepper to taste.

4. To assemble the lasagne, pour a ladleful of the cheese sauce into a rectangular ovenproof dish. Then add a layer of lasagne sheets and pour a third of the vegetable sauce over the top. Continue these three steps until the dish is full, finishing with a layer of cheese sauce. Top the dish with the grated Parmesan and cheddar cheese. Place the dish in the hot oven and bake for about 40 minutes until the top is golden brown. Alternatively, you could make individual lasagne's in separate dishes; bake these for 15 to 20 minutes or until golden brown.

Layered Aubergine & Lentil Bake

This is a fantastic alternative to lasagne and just as satisfying. Perfect with a glass of red wine.

INGREDIENTS

2 large aubergines, cut into 1cm slices lengthways

3 tablespoons olive oil

2 onions, finely chopped

3 cloves of garlic, finely chopped

250g chestnut mushrooms

Knorr herb pot (optional)

400g chopped tomatoes

140g tomato purée

Pinch of salt and sugar

2 tablespoons of dried herbs

250g Puy lentils, cooked

A handful of basil leaves

Red or green fresh chillies (optional)

250g mozzarella, sliced

100g cheddar cheese, grated

METHOD

1. Preheat the oven to 220°C.

2. Brush both sides of the aubergine slices with oil and then sprinkle with a bit of salt and leave in a colander for 10 minutes, before patting dry with kitchen paper.

3. Lay the slices on the baking sheets and bake in the oven for 15 to 20 minutes until tender, turning them halfway through.

4. Heat some oil in a large frying pan and cook the onions and garlic until soft. Then add the mushrooms, Knorr herb pot, chopped tomatoes, tomato purée, a pinch of salt and sugar, dried herbs and half a cup of water. Simmer the mixture for 10 to 15 minutes until the sauce has thickened. Add in the lentils, fresh basil and chillies if using.

5. To assemble the bake, layer the ingredients into a small baking dish, with the lentil mixture on the bottom, topped with aubergine slices, then the sliced mozzarella. Continue to repeat these steps until the dish is full, finishing with a layer of aubergine. Lastly, add the cheddar cheese to the top and bake for a further 15 to 20 minutes until the cheese is golden brown and serve with a green salad.

serves six

preparation time: 20 minutes ❖ cooking time: 40 minutes

Spinach & Four Cheese Cannelloni

A quick and easy cannelloni recipe using lasagne sheets.

INGREDIENTS

For the sauce

50g shallots, chopped

1 tablespoon rapeseed oil

350g tomato passata

1½ teaspoons mixed dried Italian herbs

250g mascarpone cheese

Salt and pepper, to taste

For the filling

75g shallots, chopped

1 tablespoon rapeseed oil

400g frozen spinach, thawed and chopped

250g ricotta cheese

40g Parmesan, grated

2 tablespoons flat leaf parsley, chopped

2 tablespoons basil leaves, chopped

Nutmeg, to taste

Salt and pepper, to taste

For the rolls

6 fresh lasagne sheets

100g mozzarella, grated

METHOD

1. Preheat the oven to 190°C. Lightly grease an ovenproof dish.

2. To make the sauce, brown the shallots in the oil, add the passata and herbs and simmer for a few minutes. Take off the heat, add the mascarpone and season with salt and pepper to taste. Pour a small amount of the sauce into the ovenproof dish and spread it around the base.

3. Start the filling by browning the shallots in the oil, then add the spinach and cook for a further 5 minutes. Meanwhile, in a separate bowl, mix the ricotta, Parmesan, parsley, basil and nutmeg. Season with salt and pepper to taste. Add to this the cooked spinach and shallots and mix again.

4. For the rolls, cut each lasagne sheet into quarters. Place a tablespoon of the ricotta mixture at the edge of each lasagne sheet and roll to make a tube. The mixture should make 24 tubes. To assemble the dish, lay the tubes side by side in the baking dish with the sauce in and spoon over the rest of the sauce to cover. Sprinkle with grated mozzarella and place in the hot oven to bake for 30 minutes. Serve with warm bread and a side salad.

Oven-Baked Red Pepper & Goat's Cheese Risotto

Creamy and comforting with no need to stir for hours on end.

INGREDIENTS

1 tablespoon olive oil

1 white onion, chopped

3 cloves of garlic, minced

1 red chilli (optional)

2 red bell peppers, chopped

225g Arborio risotto rice

120ml white wine

Salt and pepper, to taste

900ml water

Parmesan cheese, to taste

Goat's cheese, to taste

20g butter

Handful of coriander

METHOD

1. Preheat the oven to 200°C.

2. In a ovenproof pan heat the oil and fry the onion, garlic and chilli. Then add the red peppers and sauté.

3. Next add the risotto rice and fry for 1 minute ensuring all of the rice is coated.

4. Add the wine, salt and pepper then fry until the alcohol has burned off, then add around 900ml of water and bring it to the boil.

5. Cover with a lid and bake the mixture in a covered dish in the oven for 45 minutes to 1 hour. When the risotto is cooked, stir through most of the Parmesan and goat's cheese with some butter.

6. Serve immediately with a sprinkling of coriander and the remaining Parmesan cheese.

Mexican Lasagne

A Mexican take on this classic Italian dish.

INGREDIENTS

1 tablespoon olive oil
1 onion or 4 spring onions, finely chopped
1 or 2 celery stalks, finely chopped
1 carrot, finely chopped
175g sweetcorn
Half each of red, yellow and green bell peppers,
finely chopped
1 courgette, finely chopped

400g black beans, tinned
2-3 teaspoons Tex-Mex seasoning
Salt, to taste
4-6 tortilla wraps
1 pack of Uncle Ben's spicy Mexican rice
400g cheddar cheese, grated
350g pasta sauce

METHOD

1. Preheat the oven to 200°C.

2. Heat the oil in a pan and add the onion, celery, carrot, sweetcorn, peppers and courgettes then cook for 5 minutes. You want the vegetables to still have a bit of crunch. Add the black beans, taco seasoning and salt as required.

3. Grease the baking dish and line the base with a single layer of tortilla wraps. Add half of the vegetable, rice and cheese mixture. Add another single layer of tortilla wraps and top with the rest of the rice, vegetables and some cheese. Finish this with a final layer of tortilla wraps. Cover with pasta sauce and sprinkle over the remaining cheese.

4. Decorate the dish with pepper rings and tomatoes. Bake for 30 minutes, until the cheese is golden brown.

5. Serve hot with salsa, guacamole, sour cream and lettuce. For an added crunch add some crushed tortilla chips on top.

Homemade Thai Green Curry

The paste is handy to keep in the fridge for a fast weekday dinner.

INGREDIENTS

1 tablespoon vegetable oil
2 x 400g coconut milk, tinned
500g mixed vegetables cut into chunks (mushrooms, green beans, baby corn, chestnuts, broccoli, courgette or asparagus all work well)
1 teaspoon salt
1 teaspoon soft brown sugar
Handful of basil, chopped
Handful of coriander leaves, chopped
Fresh red chilli (optional)

For the green curry paste
3 green bird's eye chillies, finely chopped
1 lemon grass stalk, sliced thinly and soaked in boiling water or lime juice
1 teaspoon lime peel, shredded
1½ inches fresh ginger, peeled and chopped
1 heaped tablespoon fresh coriander
½ teaspoon roasted cumin
½ teaspoon coriander seeds
6 cloves of garlic
5 shallots, finely chopped
4 kaffir lime leaves

METHOD

1. Start by mixing all the ingredients for the curry paste in a food processor, blitzing until it becomes a paste.

2. In a medium pan, heat the oil and fry the curry paste for a few minutes. Add the coconut milk gradually until the mixture boils and starts to thicken. Add the vegetables to the pan and cook for about 10 minutes until tender.

3. Season with salt and sugar and stir. Lastly, add the red chilli and cover with the shredded basil and coriander. Serve with boiled white rice.

Sweet Potato & Black Bean Open Burrito

A healthy colourful twist on a traditional burrito.

INGREDIENTS

2 medium sweet potatoes

3-4 tablespoons yoghurt

1 teaspoon taco seasoning

Salt and pepper, to taste

400g black beans, tinned

2 tomatoes, chopped

Handful of coriander, chopped

4 tortillas, any variety

1 avocado, diced

Cheddar cheese, grated (optional)

200g sweetcorn, tinned

Jalapeños (optional)

METHOD

1. Preheat the oven to 200°C.

2. Roast the sweet potatoes in the oven for about 40 minutes, or until soft. When the potatoes have cooled, peel and mash them. Mix the mashed sweet potato with the yoghurt and taco seasoning and then season with salt and pepper.

3. In a separate bowl, mash the beans and then add the tomatoes and coriander. Lay the tortillas flat, then layer the sweet potato mixture on the tortilla and add the bean mixture on top. Top with avocado, cheese, sweetcorn and jalapeños.

4. Put the burrito back in the oven for 5 minutes. Serve with Mexican dips, such as sour cream or guacamole.

Paneer Wraps

Mildly-spiced paneer wraps for an any time snack.

INGREDIENTS

1 tablespoon sunflower oil

1 teaspoon cumin seeds

1 red onion, sliced

Fresh ginger to taste (optional)

250g paneer, grated or cut into thin strips

Salt, to taste

1 teaspoon red chilli powder or to taste

Handful of coriander, finely chopped

2 teaspoons chaat masala

2 teaspoons lemon juice

3 tortilla wraps

METHOD

1. Heat the oil in a pan. Add the cumin seeds and once they start to sizzle add in the onion. Fry for a couple of minutes until cooked but still slightly crunchy.

2. Add the ginger if required, then the paneer, salt, red chilli powder, coriander, chaat masala and lemon juice. Be careful not to overcook the paneer.

3. To serve, put the paneer mixture in a wrap and roll tightly.

Indulge
tasty & tempting delights

Blueberry Chia Pudding

A filling sweet treat perfect any time of the day.

INGREDIENTS

240ml almond milk (or any other preferred milk)

120g plain Greek yoghurt

2 tablespoons chia seeds

1 vanilla pod, seeds only

½ teaspoon cinnamon

2 teaspoons honey (or any other preferred sweetener)

20g flaked almonds

75g fresh or frozen blueberries

METHOD

1. Whisk together the milk, yoghurt, chia seeds, vanilla seeds, cinnamon and honey then leave overnight.

2. Next morning when you are ready to serve, add the almonds and blueberries.

Tip: This snack is amazingly versatile, you can use most soft fruits. Some of our favourites are mango, raspberries, grapes, strawberries and plums.

INDULGE
makes twenty to twenty five
preparation time: 15 minutes ❖ cooking time: 10 minutes

Date & Nut Rolls

❖

A great low sugar, high energy treat with no added fat.

INGREDIENTS

250g pitted dates
150g mixed nuts, roughly crushed
25g Rice Krispies
2-3 tablespoons desiccated coconut

METHOD

1. In a large pan heat the dates on a low flame until they soften. Remove from the heat and allow to cool. Then add the nuts and Rice Krispies. Mix well to combine them.

2. Roll the date mixture into round balls and coat them in the desiccated coconut and serve.

3. Alternatively, you could make long rolls and coat them in the coconut, before slicing them into half inch pieces.

4. Store the rolls in a cool place.

Baklava Tarts

A lighter alternative to traditional baklava.

INGREDIENTS

80g filo pastry sheets
150g chopped fruit and nut mix
(any combination of pistachios, walnuts, almonds,
pecans, raisins and cranberries)
1 tablespoon butter, melted

85g honey, plus more for serving
½ teaspoon ground cinnamon
Pinch of salt
Icing sugar for dusting

METHOD

1. Preheat the oven to 190°C.

2. Using a round 2-inch cookie cutter, cut rounds out of two layered sheets of filo pastry and place the double layer of cut circles into a cupcake tray.

3. Thoroughly mix the chopped fruit and nuts, melted butter, honey, cinnamon and salt.

4. Fill each pastry mould with around one teaspoon of the nut mixture.

5. Bake in the oven for 8-10 minutes, until the nuts are lightly toasted.

6. When they are cooked, remove the tarts from the cupcake tray and serve immediately with a drizzle of honey and dusting of icing sugar (optional).

Chocolate & Coconut Cookie Squares

Layer upon layer of deliciousness.

INGREDIENTS

150g digestive biscuits, made into crumbs

120g butter, melted

1 tin (397g) sweetened condensed milk

350g milk chocolate chips or dried cranberries

120g desiccated coconut

150g chopped nuts (almonds, cashews, hazelnuts)

METHOD

1. Preheat the oven to 180°C.

2. Mix the digestive biscuit crumbs and melted butter in a bowl. Transfer onto a greased baking tray (20 x 30cm) and press down to make a base.

3. Pour the sweetened condensed milk evenly over the biscuit layer. Sprinkle the chocolate chips or cranberries, coconut and nuts on top to make an even top layer and press the mixture down firmly with a fork.

4. Bake for 25 to 30 minutes or until lightly browned on top.

5. When cooked, use a knife or spatula to loosen the cookie from the sides of the pan and cut into squares while still warm.

Summer Fruit Tartlets

*A must for any afternoon tea platter
or as a sweet canapé.*

INGREDIENTS

320g sweet shortcrust pastry sheet
1 egg, beaten
100ml double cream
50g icing sugar
250g mascarpone

1 vanilla pod, seeds only
Strawberries, halved or sliced, for garnish
Whole blueberries or raspberries, for garnish
2 tablespoons apricot jam, melted
Icing sugar, for dusting

METHOD

1. Preheat the oven to 190°C.

2. Cut the pastry with round fluted cutters, cutting out as many rounds as possible. When this is done, place the pastry rounds into a greased muffin or cupcake tray, pressing the rounds into the cups with your fingers. Pierce the base of each pastry with a fork to release any trapped air and trim off any excess pastry around the edges with a knife. Brush each pastry case with beaten egg.

3. Bake the pastry cases in the hot oven for 20 minutes, until golden brown. Check the pastry halfway through to ensure that it's flat and not bubbling up; if it does bubble, prick it with a fork or press it back with your fingers. When the pastry is baked, remove the cases and place on a rack to cool. Alternatively you can buy very good ready made pastry cases from most supermarkets.

4. In a bowl, whisk the cream, sugar, mascarpone and vanilla seeds together until it forms soft peaks. When the pastry is cooled, spread the cream mixture into each case and decorate with the fruits.

5. Brush each tart with the melted apricot jam to make a glaze and then place the tarts in the fridge for at least an hour.

6. To serve, dust with some icing sugar.

Lychee & Ginger Granita

An unusual quick, easy and refreshing palate cleanser.

INGREDIENTS

1 inch piece of ginger, peeled and finely grated

125g lychees, tinned

5 fresh raspberries

Sprig of mint

METHOD

1. Place the grated ginger on to a spoon and press it down with the back of another spoon until it releases the juice.

2. Put one to one and a half teaspoons of the ginger juice in a blender with the lychees and lychee juice, then add the raspberries.

3. Liquidise the mixture and place in a container and freeze overnight.

4. A few hours before serving, remove from the freezer and scrape the granita into small crystals of ice with a fork. Reseal the container and return to the freezer.

5. Serve with a sprig of mint.

INDULGE
serves six
preparation time: 15 minutes (family version) 25 minutes (adult version)
❖ *cooking time: 30-40 minutes (family version) 1 hour 20 minutes (adult version)*

Pear, Almond & Mixed Spiced Crumble

*This humble family favourite pudding can be
transformed into a decadent adult dessert.*

INGREDIENTS

To make the crumble
100g plain flour
50g oats
100g demerara sugar
Pinch of salt
100g unsalted butter, cold
60g flaked almonds

To make the fruit
6 soft ripe pears, peeled
2 tablespoons cold water
1 teaspoon mixed spice
600ml red wine (adult version)

METHOD

1. To make the crumble, in a mixing bowl combine the flour, oats, sugar and a pinch of salt. Cut the cold butter into small cubes and add to the dry ingredients. Using your fingers rub the butter into the dry ingredients until all the big lumps disappear and the mixture turns into small crumbs.

2. **For the family version.** Preheat the oven to 180°C. Then, chop the pears into chunks and in a pan soften the pears with the spices and the water. When the pears have cooled down, place them in an oven proof dish, sprinkle the crumble topping over them and place in a hot oven for 30 minutes. Remove the crumble and sprinkle flaked almonds on the top. Return the crumble to the oven for another 15 minutes. Serve with custard, cream or ice cream.

3. **For the adult version.** Remove the core of each pear, leaving them whole and the stalk intact. Level the base of each pear so it can stand upright. Poach the pears in the red wine and mixed spice by simmering on a low heat for about 30 to 40 minutes, (cooking time will vary depending on the ripeness of the pears) until the pears are tender all the way through. While the pears are cooking, scatter the crumble mixture on to a baking tray and bake in the oven for 20 minutes, until golden brown. Toast the almonds in the oven for 10 to 15 minutes until golden brown and then mix the crumble and the almonds together. When the pears are burgundy coloured, remove from the wine and allow them to cool slightly. To serve, place the warm pears upright on a dish and scatter the pears and the dish with the crumble and almond mixture.

Pear & Chocolate Trifle

A quick but stylish chocolate dessert to impress any unexpected dinner guests.

INGREDIENTS

4 chocolate covered mini Swiss rolls

415g pears in juice, tinned, chopped

400g fresh custard

300ml whipping cream

Mixed chocolate balls or curls for decoration

Thin slices of whole fresh pear, crisped in the oven

METHOD

1. Chill four dessert glasses. In each glass slice each Swiss roll into five pieces and arrange them on the bottom and sides of the glass.

2. Add some of the pear juice to the glass to soften the Swiss roll. Next, add chopped pears until the glass is about one third full. Pour a layer of custard into the glass, stopping when it's about two thirds full.

3. In a separate bowl, whip the cream until firm. Fill each glass to the top with the whipped cream. When the trifles have been assembled refrigerate them for a few hours.

4. To serve, decorate with the chocolate curls or balls and a slice of crisped pear.

Salted Caramel Kulfi

A traditional Indian ice cream with a modern flavour.

INGREDIENTS

360ml full-fat milk
170ml condensed milk
120ml double cream
3 tablespoons salted caramel sauce

Serving options
Flaked almonds
Crushed nuts
Chocolate chips

METHOD

1. Mix the milk, condensed milk, cream and salted caramel sauce together. Make sure you combine all the ingredients well.

2. Pour the mixture into moulds of your choice and freeze for 6 to 8 hours, or until set.

3. To serve, remove the kulfi from the moulds and sprinkle them with flaked almonds, crushed nuts or chocolate chips.

Cookies & Cream Cheesecake

An easy to make, no bake cheesecake that's loved by young and old alike.

INGREDIENTS

308g Oreo cookies (2 packets), additional for decoration if required
50g unsalted butter, melted
500g full fat cream cheese

1 teaspoon vanilla extract
500ml double cream
2 tablespoons icing sugar

METHOD

1. Separate the 2 packets of Oreos as follows:
   18 Oreos for the base.
   6 Oreos for the cheesecake filling.
   4 Oreos for the top layer.

2. Next, separate all the Oreos from the cream filling, and set this to one side, keeping the Oreos in their respective quantities

3. Crush the 18 Oreos for the base and put into a loose bottomed cake tin (8-inch diameter). Add the melted butter and mix well. Flatten the mixture and set aside.

4. To the Oreo cream filling add the icing sugar, cream cheese and vanilla extract. Whisk well. Once this mixture is fully-combined (some lumps may still remain), add the double cream and whisk again until the mixture becomes thick. Break up the 6 Oreos for the cheesecake filling into small pieces, folding them in carefully.

5. Pour the cream mixture onto the base and spread it out as evenly as you can. Finally, make a fine crumb from the remaining 4 Oreos, and sprinkle this on top of the cheesecake filling to form a thin layer on the very top of the cheesecake.
   Place the cheesecake in the fridge for about 4 hours until it is firm enough to serve. The cheesecake can be decorated with extra Oreos just before serving.

Churros

Look what you can make at home now...

INGREDIENTS

50g salted butter
1 teaspoon vanilla essence
350ml boiling water
250g plain flour
Pinch of salt

1 teaspoon baking powder
100g caster sugar
2 teaspoons cinnamon
Sunflower oil, for frying

METHOD

1. Place the butter and vanilla extract into the boiling water, stir until the butter has melted into the water and set aside.

2. In a large mixing bowl, combine the flour, salt and baking powder. Add the water and butter to the dry ingredients and stir until the mixture is smooth and lump free. The batter should be thicker than a liquid but looser than dough.

3. Rest the mixture for a minimum of 10 to 15 minutes.

4. Meanwhile, mix the caster sugar and cinnamon together and set aside for later.

5. To cook the batter, put it into a piping bag and, using a 1½-2cm star nozzle, pipe strips about 10cm long directly into a pan of oil on a medium heat. Deep fry the strips for a few minutes, stirring intermittently, until the churros are golden.

6. Remove them from the pan and place onto a paper towel to drain. Sprinkle with the cinnamon sugar to taste. Serve with either melted chocolate, or salted caramel sauce.

Malty Rocky Road Bites

A moreish blend of creamy chocolate and crunchy biscuit.

INGREDIENTS

100g butter

4 tablespoons golden syrup

200g milk chocolate, broken into chunks

225g digestive biscuits, roughly crushed

225g Maltesers

Orange-flavoured chocolate for topping (optional)

METHOD

1. Put the butter, syrup and milk chocolate into a microwavable dish or a pan on the hob. Melt in short bursts in the microwave or over a low heat on the hob until fully melted.

2. Add the biscuit crumbs to the chocolate and mix well. Then add the Maltesers and give it all another mix to ensure they are well incorporated. Pour the mix into a baking tin or tray, lined with baking paper (approx. 9 x 7 inch or equivalent) making sure the mixture is pressed down and pushed into the corners.

3. Lastly, layer or drizzle some melted orange chocolate on top if you like. To set the mixture, pop in the fridge for a few hours. Serve sliced into squares.

Chocolate Volcano Pudding

Go for it... life's too short!

INGREDIENTS

140g dark chocolate

120g unsalted butter

4 eggs

120g caster sugar

30g plain flour

4 oven-safe ramekins, greased

METHOD

1. Preheat the oven to 180°C.

2. Gently melt the chocolate on a low power in the microwave.

3. Mix the butter into the chocolate, stirring until melted.

4. Whisk together the eggs and the sugar and add to the chocolate mix. Add in the flour until the mixture is smooth and gooey.

5. Pour the mixture into ramekins.

6. To bake, place the ramekins in a hot oven for 8-10 minutes until cooked on the outside but still gooey on the inside.

7. Serve warm with your favourite ice cream.

Chutney Recipes

Easy Green Coriander Chutney

Makes half a cup

INGREDIENTS

150g coriander, chopped
2 green chillies (or to taste), roughly chopped
1½ teaspoons lemon juice

1 tablespoon sugar
4 tablespoons grated coconut
Salt, to taste

METHOD

1. Combine all the above ingredients with a little water and then blend to make a smooth mixture.

2. Store in a container and keep refrigerated.

Red Chilli & Garlic Chutney

Makes half a cup

INGREDIENTS

10 dried red chillies, stems and seeds removed
120ml boiling hot water
10 cloves of garlic

¼ teaspoon sugar
2 teaspoons lemon juice
Salt, to taste

METHOD

1. Soak the red chillies in the boiling water for about half an hour. After the chillies have soaked, add all the remaining ingredients to the chillies and water and grind to a smooth paste.

2. Store in a container and keep refrigerated.

Date & Tamarind Chutney

Makes half a cup

INGREDIENTS

280g dates, deseeded and chopped
2-3 tablespoons tamarind, deseeded
150g jaggery, grated
480ml water

½ teaspoon red chilli powder
1 teaspoon ground cumin
Salt, to taste

METHOD

1. Put the dates, tamarind and jaggery in a pan with 480ml of water and simmer for 20 to 25 minutes until soft. Leave this to cool and once cooled strain the mixture through a sieve.

2. Stir in the red chilli powder, ground cumin and salt.

3. Use as required. Store in an airtight container and keep refrigerated.

Coconut Chutney

Makes 1 cup

INGREDIENTS

For the chutney
60g fresh coconut, grated
2 green chillies, chopped
1 teaspoon grated ginger
1 tablespoon roasted split gram lentils
Salt, to taste

For the tempering
1 teaspoon oil
½ teaspoon split black lentils (urad dal), dehusked
½ teaspoon mustard seeds
1 whole red chilli, broken in half
2-3 curry leaves

METHOD

1. For the chutney, put the coconut, green chillies, ginger, roasted split gram lentils and salt into a blender with a little water and grind to make a fine paste. Set aside.

2. Prepare the tempering by heating the oil in a small pan. Add the mustard seeds, split lentils, red chilli and curry leaves and stirring until the mustard seeds crackle. Pour over the chutney and mix well.

3. Keep refrigerated.

Tip: To make coconut chutney creamier add two tablespoons of yoghurt.

Sweet
C H I L L I
Friday

@PeppercornPassion

©2018 Meze Publishing Ltd &
Peppercorn Passion Ltd. All rights reserved.

First edition printed in 2018 in the UK.

ISBN: 978-1-910863-38-1

*Authors: Deepa Jaitha, Alpa Lakhani,
Sangita Manek, Sheetal Mistry, Sonia Sapra
and Anjana Soneji-Natalia Peppercorn Passion Ltd.*

Edited by: Katie Fisher & Muirne Cunning

Designed by: Alana Bishop & Paul Cocker

Photography by: Xavier Buendia

Additional photography by: Rupen Lakhani

*Contributors: Phil Turner, Anna Tebble, Faye Bailey,
Sarah Koriba, Hannah Keith, Ella Michele,
David Wilson, Amy Clarke*

me:ze
PUBLISHING

Published by Meze Publishing Limited
Unit 1b, 2 Kelham Square
Kelham Riverside
Sheffield S3 8SD
Web: www.mezepublishing.co.uk
Telephone: 0114 275 7709
Email: info@mezepublishing.co.uk